The Boys' Book of Survival

HOW TO SURVIVE ANYTHING, ANYWHERE

Written by Guy Campbell
Illustrated by Simon Ecob
Edited by Rachel Carter
Designed by Zoe Quayle
With thanks to Toby Buchan
and Philippa Wingate

The Boys' Book of Survival

HOW TO SURVIVE ANYTHING, ANYWHERE

Buster Books

First published in Great Britain in 2008 by Buster Books,
an imprint of Michael O'Mara Books Limited,
9 Lion Yard, Tremadoc Road, London SW4 7NQ

Cover design by Angie Allison
(from an original design by www.blacksheep-uk.com)
Cover illustration by Paul Moran

Papers used by Buster Books are natural, recyclable products made
from wood grown in sustainable forests. The manufacturing processes
conform to the environmental regulations of the country of origin.

A CIP catalogue record for this book is available from
the British Library.

ISBN: 978-1-906082-12-3

2 4 6 8 10 9 7 5 3

www.mombooks.com/busterbooks

Printed and bound in England by Clays Ltd, St Ives plc

WARNING

The survival techniques in this book are for use only in emergencies. Take a responsible adult with you if you go on an expedition, because it is never a good idea to undertake any of the activities described by yourself.

We urge you at all times to make yourself aware of and obey all laws, regulations and local byelaws and respect all rights, including the rights of landowners, and all relevant laws protecting animals and plants and controlling the carrying and use of implements such as catapults and knives.

DISCLAIMER

The publisher and the author disclaim all liability, as far as is legally permitted, for accidents or injuries or loss of any nature that may occur as a result of the use or misuse of the information and guidance given in this book.

Above all, exercise common sense, particularly when fire or sharp objects are involved, and follow at all times safety precautions and advice from responsible adults. That said, it is fun to learn new skills, and they may one day be useful.

CONTENTS

HOW TO PLAN A GROUP EXPEDITION

'Expedition' is the word used to describe a trip with a purpose. Here are some tips on how to make sure any expedition you and your team embark upon is well planned and goes without a hitch.

1. The first thing to do when planning an expedition is to come up with a 'mission statement'. This is a couple of sentences that clearly describe where you are going on the trip, why you are going, and what you want to achieve when you are away.

Here is a sample mission statement:
'I plan to lead my team through the Atlas Mountains in Morocco. We will observe the hill tribes living there, and take some fantastic photos of the people and the landscape.'

2. Use a map to plan your route to and from your destination. Work out how far your team can travel each day and plan where you will camp each night. Plan at least one alternative route both there and back in case you come across any obstacles on your journey.

3. Study books about previous expeditions to the area. Read and compare the accounts of least three different people. Then make notes on the following points:

a) What type of weather you can expect? Decide on a start date and an end date for your expedition. Investigate the type of weather you can expect in the area at that time of year as this will affect the clothing and camping equipment you will need to take.

b) What type of ground you will be covering? Is the terrain flat or mountainous? Do you need to take ropes and climbing gear, or would it be wiser to take cross-country skis?

c) Are there any natural sources of food or water along your planned route? How many days will you need to travel before you reach them? This will affect your calculations of how many days' food and drink rations you need to carry at the beginning of your journey.

d) Are there any deadly creatures you should watch out for along the way, such as snakes or poisonous spiders? This will influence the medical supplies you pack.

4. Make a list of everything that could go wrong on the expedition. What if someone fell ill from food poisoning or broke a leg? Make a list of the supplies and equipment you'd need to deal with each situation.

5. Match each member of your team with essential duties. These duties might include map-reading, shelter-building, monitoring rations, fetching water, cooking, gathering wood and building fires, keeping the camp clean, and watching out for dangerous animals.

6. Use all the information you have gathered to write up a 'trip plan'. Give a copy of the plan to everyone who will be going on the expedition. Leave a copy with someone who is not. This person can alert the emergency services if you do not return on time.

HOW TO MAKE YOUR OWN SURVIVAL PACK

The equipment you take with you will depend on the type of expedition you are planning. But whether you are camping in the wilderness, hiking through mountains or trekking through jungle, there are some expedition essentials that will keep you warm, dry and well fed.

ESSENTIAL ITEMS

• Water (as much as you can carry) • Water purifying tablets • Food rations (including high-energy food, such as chocolate and nuts) • Maps • A good compass • Warm clothing (including a hat) • Hiking boots • A waterproof coat • Camping equipment: tent, sleeping bag, cooking utensils • A first-aid kit • A whistle • A flashlight (with spare bulb and batteries) • A pocket knife with a selection of heads (legally, the blade must be non-locking, and must fold away and be no longer than 7.5 cm) • A waterproof sheet 1.5 m by 2 m • Wristwatch • Sturdy plastic bags for carrying water • Fish hooks and twine • Mobile phone • Waterproof matches, a lighter and tinder • Magnifying glass (which can be used to start a fire) • A candle • At least 8 m of cord • Wire for making snares • Insect repellent • Sunscreen • Emergency blanket

BEFORE YOU LEAVE

• Check that all your electrical appliances are working and fully charged, or have new batteries before you set off.

• Take a 'survival bag' with you. This is a large, brightly coloured waterproof bag that you can sleep in if necessary.

• Even if your expedition should only take you a couple of hours, pack the equipment and rations you would need to survive for at least twenty-four hours in an emergency.

HOW TO BE A GOOD LEADER

There may be a time when you find yourself with a group of people in a potentially dangerous situation. Someone needs to take the lead – and that someone could be you. Here are some things to remember if you step forward for the role of leader.

MAKE A STRONG START

When you first meet the members of your team make eye contact with each of them. This gives an excellent first impression. A confident, firm (but not too firm) handshake helps, too. Stand upright with your shoulders back. This will give your teammates confidence in your abilities. If you slouch you will look uninterested and nervous – not obvious leadership qualities.

Try really hard to remember everyone's name and repeat it back to them as you introduce yourself: 'Hello Jack, I'm James.' This will make people feel you're interested in them and they will be more likely to trust you.

BE GOOD AT SOMETHING

People often admire someone who is good at something. If you read this book from cover to cover, your excellent survival knowledge will be sure to impress your team. Sporting talent is impressive, but if you lack athletic prowess don't worry, metalworking and woodworking skills are really useful in survival situations. Failing that, make sure you have the right equipment for an expedition. Being the owner of the biggest and the best tools is always a plus.

If all else fails, be witty and charming. Many leaders get to the top by putting people at ease and making them laugh.

ALWAYS TRY TO REMAIN POSITIVE

• When in a difficult situation, try to see solutions to the problems that face you rather than moaning about them. Complaining wastes time and can lower your team's spirits. Try to keep your worries and anxieties to yourself.

• Keep any criticism to a minimum. Let's face it, nobody's perfect. If you are slow to blame people when things go wrong and quick to praise them if they perform a task well, your teammates will stay keen and cooperative.

• Don't ask anyone to perform any chores or take any risks that you wouldn't be happy to take on yourself.

- When one of your comrades is speaking to you, pay careful attention to what they are saying. Being aware and making use of your team's varied talents and expertise can only get you ahead.

- Don't have favourites. Make sure everyone feels that they are a valued member of the team.

HOW TO AVOID PIRANHAS

If you find yourself on an expedition in a South American rainforest and you have no choice but to cross a river, spare a thought for piranhas. You've heard of these ferocious fish with razor-sharp teeth who have a frightening reputation for stripping the flesh off animals, right down to their bare bones. Piranhas can grow to 50 cm in length, so they are not ideal swimming companions.

Here are some tips for keeping the flesh on your bones where it belongs.

PIRANHA POINTERS

- Throw a dead animal, such as a goat or sheep, into the water downstream from where you want to cross. The carcass will attract the piranhas and give you some time to cross, but not much. If the shoal is big and hungry enough, it will demolish a dead goat in a few minutes and you will be next on the menu.

- Piranhas live in warm waters that are still or flow slowly. Make sure the point at which you attempt to cross the river is one where the water is cold or fast moving.

• Wait until dark before attempting to cross as this is when piranhas are least active. Then swim or wade smoothly through the water, keeping any splashing to a minimum so as not to alert the piranhas to your presence.

DON'T PANIC

Piranhas don't go out of their way to attack humans unless they are really hungry. They are most dangerous during dry seasons, when water levels are low and food is hard to come by. So you might want to set up camp and wait until another time of year to get cross that river!

HOW TO SURVIVE A TORNADO

Tornadoes, also known as 'twisters', are windstorms that create a highly destructive, whirling funnel of air. They cause devastating damage to the areas they hit and happen very quickly, with little warning.

PREPARATION

The best way to survive a tornado is to be prepared for it. If you live in an area that is prone to tornadoes, keep an eye on the weather by regularly logging onto a weather website, or tuning into TV or radio weather forecasts.

Keep a 'tornado kit' in a metal box inside your house. The kit should include a mobile phone, a portable radio, first-aid supplies, a bell, horn or whistle for signalling, and a flashlight.

Additional supplies should include food, water, batteries and protective clothing. Keep your tornado kit somewhere handy so you can grab it easily if a twister hits.

EARLY WARNING SIGNS

Here are some signs that you can look out for that will tell you if a twister is heading your way.

- Often you will hear a tornado coming before you see it. Listen out for a sound like a waterfall that turns into a roar as it gets closer. The sound of a tornado has been compared to that of a train or even a jet engine.

- The sky often turns a sickly greenish or greenish-black colour just before a storm hits.

- It may suddenly start to hail.

- You may notice clouds that are moving very fast, perhaps twisting into a cone shape.

- You might see debris, such as dust, branches and leaves, dropping from the sky.

When the tornado arrives, you can expect to see a funnel-shaped cloud that is spinning rapidly. Debris will be pulled upwards into the funnel.

GET INSIDE

The best place to be when a tornado arrives is inside. Houses in areas that are prone to tornadoes often have 'storm cellars' underneath them. These are the safest places to hide. If the building you're in does not have a cellar, head for the lowest floor. Find the smallest room on that floor, such as a bathroom or cupboard. If that's not possible, look for a room in the middle of the house with no windows. A hallway may provide the best shelter.

Close any doors and windows that are located on the same side of the room as the approaching tornado. Open all the doors and windows on the other side of the room. This will help prevent the powerful wind from entering the building. Tornadoes have been known to pick up entire buildings.

Take shelter under some solid furniture, such as a heavy kitchen table. If you are in a bathroom jump into the bathtub. Cover yourself with a mattress, a sofa, towels or anything soft that you can get your hands on to protect yourself from flying debris.

SURVIVING OUTSIDE

If you are unlucky enough to be caught outside without buildings near by, try to get out of the path of the tornado by moving to the side, rather than trying to outrun it.

Never hide behind a tree or climb into a car, caravan or tractor, as these may be sucked up by the tornado.

If the only shelter you can find is in a ditch or hollow, make sure you lie face down and use your arms to protect your head and neck.

HOW TO CHOOSE A GOOD PLACE TO SHELTER

If you find yourself stranded in an unfamiliar environment, your top priority is to find a safe place to sleep. Well before darkness falls, you need to find a suitable place to shelter.

TAKE COVER

The most important thing a shelter provides is protection from the elements. In desert areas you will need to stay out of the sun. In mountains or polar regions rain, snow and wind will seriously threaten your chances of survival.

Caves provide good natural shelter. Always check them out carefully first – you don't want to find you are sharing your new-found home with a surprised wild animal, such as a hibernating bear or a mountain lion. Scout around for tell-tale signs that the cave may be occupied. These include bones, nests or droppings inside or near the cave entrance, and clumps of vegetation that are being used as bedding.

If you can't find a cave, look for a spot that is shielded from the elements. Camping at the base of rockfaces and cliffs will offer some shelter. However, check that there aren't any loose rocks lying around, as these would suggest you are in danger from falling debris.

THE IDEAL SPOT

A clearing in a wood is the ideal spot to make camp, especially if there is a fast-running stream near by. That way you will have building materials for your shelter, wood for your fire and water for drinking, washing and cooking.

PLACES TO AVOID

When looking for a place to set up camp here are some places to avoid:

- Stay away from areas close to ponds or lakes. Water that isn't flowing attracts insects that might bite or sting you.

- Don't camp in a hollow at the bottom of a hill. Rain water may run off the hillside and flood your shelter.

- Avoid sheltering beside a cliff or rockface in snowy terrain, as this is where snow may build up and it could bury you while you sleep. There might also be a danger of avalanches.

- Never camp at the top of a hill as this will be exposed to the wind and rain. Your shelter could easily be blown away.

HOW TO SURVIVE FALLING OFF A HORSE

Horses have a habit of not doing quite what you want, and this occasionally includes dumping you on the ground. You are more likely to survive in one piece if you learn how to take a tumble.

1. Never mount your trusty steed without the right safety gear. A riding helmet could save your life. Wearing jeans and a tough long-sleeved jacket will protect your arms and legs from being scratched by low branches or being grazed if you fall on rough ground.

2. Once you have realized you are unfortunate enough to have chosen a horse that is impossible to control and that falling off is inevitable, try to look for a soft patch of ground to land on. It's better to fall off sooner onto sand, soil or grass rather than later onto rocks or gravel.

3. As you begin to fall, it is important to accept that you and your horse are going to part company for a while. Don't cling on for dear life. Kick your feet out of the stirrups and drop the reins to ensure that you aren't dragged cross-country for miles.

4. As you fall, try not to tense up. Keep your limbs as floppy as possible. Resist the temptation to throw your arms straight out in front of you to break your fall. The only thing you will break is your bones. The more relaxed your body is, the better your landing will be.

5. As you fall, try to propel yourself as far away from your horse as you can to avoid being trampled under its hooves.

6. Ideally you should attempt to land on your feet, bending you knees immediately on impact. Then curl into a ball and roll away from your horse to stop your vital organs hitting the ground. Cover your head and neck with your arms to protect your head.

7. Don't jump up as soon as you have rolled to a standstill. One by one test your fingers, arms, legs and especially your neck for damage by gently moving them. If everything seems intact get up very slowly. If you are injured any sharp movements could make matters worse.

The good news is that you are in one piece. The bad news is that your horse is a mile away – and it probably won't be the last time you take a tumble.

HOW TO SURVIVE A DUEL

Imagine you wake up on a Monday morning and, instead of opening your eyes and seeing your messy bedroom, you find yourself transported back in time to the 17th century. Superb sword-fighting skills would be essential to your chances of survival.

SURVIVAL SKILL WARNING:

Never, ever pick up a real sword in the 21st century. Even in the 17th century, duelling was a last resort.

TOOLS OF THE TRADE

If you are right-handed hold your sword in your right hand and vice versa if you are left-handed. Your sword is thin and whippy, so you shouldn't need to hold it with both hands.

THE 'EN GARDE' POSITION

Every musketeer knows the foundation of all good sword-fighting moves is a steady 'en garde' position. En garde allows the fighter to switch quickly between defending themselves or attacking their opponent.

Here's how it is done:

1. Stand one large step away from being able to touch your opponent's outstretched sword. Any closer and if your strike misses, you will be left standing in your enemy's strike range. Make sure your back is to the

sun – that way your enemy's body will be well lit, but
yours will be hidden in shadow.

2. Turn your body to the side. Right-handers: point your
right foot directly towards the opponent, keeping your
left foot where it is (left-handers vice versa).

3. Bend your knees so that your body is well balanced.

4. Keeping your back as straight as possible, bend your
sword arm at the elbow. Hold the handle (called the
grip) of your sword level with your hips, with the point
level with your head but slanting away from your body-
towards your enemy. This 'stance' will ensure your body
is protected from your head to your hips.

5. Hold your other hand behind your back, or to one
side, so it doesn't get in your way. You should feel well
balanced and comfortable in this position.

TACTICS

As your opponent attempts to strike, straighten your arm
and go in for the attack. Try to knock aside his sword with
your own blade. Then quickly step forward and counter
his strike with your own. Any strike is a good strike. Your
opponent's legs, arms and even his hands are often easier
to target than his torso.

When fighting, conserve energy by keeping your
movements to a minimum. Let your opponent do all the
running around. He will soon tire. If you can, back him
into furniture and make him fall over. When he is on the
ground and swordless, you can afford to be chivalrous and
let him leave unharmed.

HOW TO SURVIVE AN ALIEN INVASION

No one is really sure what aliens look like. However, many people believe that they do exist and one day you might well come face-to-face with one. If you meet an alien, whether it is a little green man, a tall purple woman, or a shapeless blob of talking mucus, be very careful. It may be a tourist alien, here on Earth for two weeks to see the sights and soak up some of our oxygen-rich atmosphere. However, it could be scouting for a forthcoming alien invasion.

JUST VISITING

If you're lucky enough to have bumped into an alien tourist it's a great opportunity to make extraterrestrial friends with it. Be as charming as possible, no matter how revolting it looks, and it may invite you to its home planet in return. Show it the sights – point out that Earth only has one sun, that it has one moon orbiting it, and that our sky is blue. Some planets have many moons and different- coloured skies so be prepared for it to find this quite odd.

Be hospitable. You don't want the alien returning home to its planet, telling terrible stories about how horrible Earthlings are and then coming back with all its friends and family to either take over or destroy the Earth.

WORLD DOMINATION

Of course, if this alien is planning to take over the world it will not have much time for chit-chat. It will probably say something like: 'Bow down inferior Earthling. You stand before the Emperor Zog. Prepare to meet your doom.' In this case run like the wind and alert the authorities so they can impose a state of national emergency. If, however, your path is blocked by the spacecraft parked on your doorstep, try holding up a mirror in front of your extraterrestrial visitor. It will never have seen its reflection, so this is guaranteed to baffle it completely, and keep it busy until help arrives.

SURVIVE THE INVASION

Aliens usually start their invasions in capital cities because lots of powerful people work there. Gather together your friends and family and head away from the cities as soon as you hear of the invasion. Besides, fighting an alien invasion is best left to the professionals.

Take a radio with you so you can keep up to date with the latest alien movements and listen out for the all-clear. Choose a place to hide that is as remote as possible so that you can stay out of the invaders' way.

All you need to do now is wait for Earth's armed forces to win the day, or for the aliens to get tired of the Earth's changeable weather and go home. Aliens do not like the rain and will do their utmost to avoid a shower. A few good thunderstorms should send them packing.

Top Tip: Aliens might try to pose as humans. So look out for unusual behaviour in your loved ones. Avoid people with glowing eyes or weird-sounding voices – anyone showing confusion when performing simple human tasks such as opening doors and putting on clothes is also a dead giveaway.

HOW TO SURVIVE A BULLY

Unfortunately, bullies crop up in many different places, from playgrounds to street corners. Some people just seem to like to tease and scare others to make themselves feel stronger and more important. Here are some tips to help you if you are unlucky enough to come across a bully.

DON'T SUFFER IN SILENCE

Being bullied is a really miserable experience, so don't just grin and bear it. Tell someone in authority, such as a teacher or parent, exactly what is happening and let them deal with the bully.

Write down exactly what the bully says or does, and make a note of any witnesses to the bullying. That way you can give an adult an accurate account of what happened.

A bully will seek out victims who appear insecure or scared. Some people find that taking martial arts or self-defence classes helps them feel more confident. However, never use violence against bullies. Beating them up might seem like an attractive option, but in reality it will only make things worse. Leave their punishment to those in authority.

Try not to show the bully you are intimidated or hurt by their behaviour. Counter their jeering and taunting with a smile or a joke. Don't attempt sarcasm or jokes at the bully's expense, however. That will just give them more reason to continue harassing you. Often a bully who doesn't get a reaction will get bored and leave you alone.

HOW TO SURVIVE A SHARK ATTACK

Unsurprisingly, the best way to survive a shark attack is to avoid sharks in the first place. While the danger of being attacked by a shark is hugely exaggerated in many movies (you are statistically more likely to be killed by a hippopotamus than a shark), swimming in shark-infested water isn't a smart thing to do. However, if you do find yourself among fishy friends, take these precautions to minimize your chances of becoming a shark snack.

DOS AND DON'TS

• Sharks like to eat fish. Stay away from fishing boats and groups of sea birds where sharks are likely to be hunting.

• If you cut yourself, get out of the water immediately. Sharks can smell blood from a long way off and will soon come to investigate what is causing the delicious smell.

• Try to swim with a group of people. Sharks are less likely to attack if they are outnumbered. Also, the more people there are keeping an eye out for fins breaking the water, the safer you will be.

• Wear dark, plain colours. Brightly coloured bathing costumes or wetsuits and even shiny watches and jewellery may catch the light and make you look like a tasty exotic fish.

• Never provoke a shark by lunging at it or waving your arms and legs around. If a shark feels threatened, it is much more likely to attack.

ACTION IF ATTACKED

If a shark has decided to attack, it will begin to dart to and fro, zig-zagging and lifting its head. Here's what to do:

• Swim away as quickly as you can and get out of the water. If you can't, stay calm. Don't thrash and splash about – the shark will think that you're injured and an easy kill.

• Try to get into a position where your back is protected by rocks, a reef, or by another swimmer. That way you can concentrate on defending yourself from the front.

• When the shark attacks, don't freeze with fear. Hit it with a sharp object or your fists. Aim your blows at its eyes, gills or at the end of its nose, which are its most sensitive areas.

HOW TO MAKE A LADDER

Here's a quick and easy way of making a ladder. The type of knot you need to use is called a 'manharness hitch.' You will need two equal lengths of sturdy rope and several short but tough lengths of a branch.

1. Put a loop in one rope.

2. The bottom of the rope crosses over the loop as shown here.

3. Put a twist in the top of the loop.

4. Take the twist over the bottom of the rope and tuck it through the bottom of your loop.

5. Push a length of branch into the new loop. Tug on the rope so the knot takes shape and is tight.

6. Repeat the knots at intervals on this and the other rope to make a ladder.

Important: Test the strength of your ladder before using it.

HOW TO AVOID BEING ATTACKED BY A POLAR BEAR

Polar bears rarely attack humans, preferring a diet of seals and fish to human flesh. However, they're strong and very curious, so it is best to take precautions to avoid attack.

POLAR PRECAUTIONS

• Visit the South Pole not the North Pole. Polar bears only live in the Arctic Circle, so you'll be out of paws' reach.

• When possible sleep in concrete buildings. Polar bears have claws that can grow up to 13 cm long, and will make short work of a tent. Male bears can weigh up to half a tonne and would flatten a wooden hut with ease.

• Polar bears have an excellent sense of smell. Always keep your camp clean and tidy. The smell of rubbish will attract hungry bears from miles around.

• Stay away from dead animals you find on the ice.
A bear may be near by looking for an easy meal and
if he sees you he might prefer fresh meat.

• If you do encounter a polar bear, never turn and run.
Stand up in front of it holding your coat or a blanket
over your head to make yourself look bigger than you are.
Wave your arms around and make as much noise as
possible. With luck the bear will decide you are too difficult
a meal to bother with and head off for a seal snack.

HOW TO SURVIVE A LONG CAR JOURNEY

When you're stuck in the back of the car on the way to
visit your relations, boredom can strike at any time. Make
sure you survive the trip.

WHAT NOT TO DO

• Don't kick the back of the seat in front of you over
and over again.

• Avoid singing the following song over and over again:
'I know a song that'll get on your nerves,
get on your nerves, get your nerves.
I know a song that'll get on your nerves,
here's how it goes . . .' (repeat)

• Resist asking any of the following questions:
'Are we nearly there yet?', 'Is it far now?',
'When's lunch/dinner/breakfast?'

- Don't try to climb into the front seat from the back seat when the car is moving.

- Don't have a back-seat burping contest. However bored you are, it's in your best interests not to distract the driver from the road ahead.

GAME ON

Give these games a go and keep yourself entertained for hours (if not days).

The Number-Plate Game: This is a classic car-journey game, which can be played with any number of players. Simply start with the letter 'A' and take turns to look for number plates containing 'B', 'C', 'D' and so on. Although it's tempting, don't ask the driver to speed up simply for you to check out the number plate in front.

In-Car Bingo: Prepare a bingo sheet in advance for each person to work from. Offer a prize to the first person to spot all the items on their sheet. They may get to choose the radio station for the next half hour or decide where to stop for snacks next.

HOW TO READ AN ORIENTEERING COMPASS

1. Hold the compass out flat so that the needle can spin around freely.

2. Stand still for a few moments until the north-seeking end of the needle (usually marked with red paint) settles in one position – this is magnetic north.

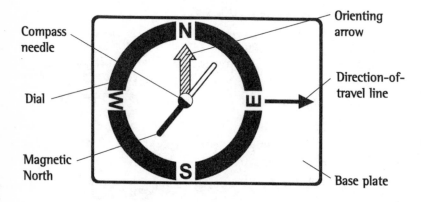

Orienting arrow

Compass needle

Dial

Magnetic North

Direction-of-travel line

Base plate

3. Keep the compass level and turn the dial until the orienting mark for north is over the coloured end of the needle. Now you know exactly which way south, east and west are, too.

Top Tip: Try not to stand too close to any large metal objects as these may affect the compass reading. Also, if you happen to have a magnet in your pocket the needle will point to that rather than finding north, which won't help at all if you are lost.

Once you've learned how to read a compass you'll be able to use it to find your way even when there are no visible landmarks to take your bearings from. If you are out walking and want to set up camp that evening at the base of a hill in the distance, follow the instructions below.

1. Aim the compass so that the arrow indicating the direction-of-travel is pointing directly at the hill.

2. With the arrow still aimed at the hill turn the dial until the orienting mark for north is over the north end of the compass needle.

3. Using these bearings you'll be able to follow the direction-of-travel line towards the hill, even if you have to walk through a forest – just walk towards the hill, keeping the needle firmly positioned on the mark for north.

HOW TO COPE WITHOUT A COMPASS

If you are unfortunate enough to have forgotten your compass all is not lost – as long as someone is wearing a wristwatch you'll be able to use the sun to work out which way is north.

The sun rises in the east and sets in the west wherever you are. However, did you know that at 12 noon in the northern hemisphere the sun is due south and at 12 noon in the southern hemisphere it is due north?

To find south in the northern hemisphere: hold your watch horizontally and aim the hour hand directly at the sun. The point on the watch face between 12 o'clock and the hour hand is due south.

To find north in the southern hemisphere: aim 12 o'clock on the watch face at the sun and then divide the angle between the hour hand and 12. This gives you the direction of north.

Northern hemisphere

Top Tip: If you only have a digital watch with you simply draw a clock face on a piece of paper. Find out the time on your digital watch and mark where the hands would be on an analogue clock on your picture. Then follow the instructions above.

HOW TO MAKE A COMPASS USING THE SUN

You can still work out roughly which direction is which, even without a compass or a watch, just by using the movement of the sun. You need a little bit of time to get this right.

You will need:

• A long, straight stick • Two medium-sized pebbles
• Some level ground • A piece of string and a twig

1. Place the stick in the ground and mark the tip of the stick's shadow in the morning with one pebble.

2. Draw a semi-circular line around the stick (use a piece of string tied to the stick and a twig at the other end to mark the ground). The line should be the same distance away from the stick as the pebble.

3. The stick's shadow will get shorter as the time gets closer to 12 noon, and longer as the afternoon goes on. Wait until the stick's shadow touches the edge of the semi-circle again and mark the point with your second pebble.

4. As the sun moves across the sky from east to west the shadow from the stick will move in the opposite direction, from west to east. The line between your morning pebble and your evening pebble marks a line from west to east, so if you draw another line at a right angle to this, you will also have north and south.
(Remember north and south are reversed in the southern hemisphere.)

HOW TO SURVIVE A HAUNTING

Whether or not you personally believe in ghosts, some people certainly do. They will swear that things happen in their houses that are hard to explain – objects move, there are strange noises, cold areas in rooms, or they even catch glimpses of the ghosts themselves.

Perhaps you feel fine or even excited about having a ghost in your house. This is useful when surviving a haunting because experts believe that making friends with a ghost is the best way to stop it doing annoying things around your house.

Talking to the ghost is a positive thing to do. Some say that ghosts are confused and unsure of why they are stuck on Earth. Try reminding the ghost that it has loved ones waiting for it 'on the other side'. This might spur it into moving on. Or you can try simply telling the ghost in a loud voice that you'd like it to leave. You never know, it might be a timid spirit who is easily spooked.

OUT OUT OUT

If giving the ghost a good talking-to doesn't work, take a lit candle and a silver bell into every room in the house. Walk to each corner of each room with the candle in one hand and ring the bell with the other.

Next take the candle and the bell outside and visit each corner of the house, too. This supposedly has the effect of chasing the ghost out of any corner it has become comfortable in.

ANTI-SPOOK DEVICES

Other ways of making the house ghost-unfriendly include sprinkling a thin line of sea salt along each window sill and doorway, scattering rice on the kitchen floor overnight, painting your front door red and placing your shoes on the floor before you go to bed so that they point in different directions.

Try all these at once and the ghosts will probably leave your house and stay away for good – as will all your friends, who will think you are crazy . . .

HOW TO ESCAPE TRICKY SITUATIONS

You are mistaken for a spy and seized by undercover agents. You are tied up with rope and bundled into the boot of a car. Here's what you need to do:

THE ROPE ESCAPE

It is important to start your escape while being tied up. The trick is to make your body take up as much space as possible. Draw your arms into your body and hunch your shoulders. Breathe in deeply and swell your chest out. Flex and expand your muscles as much as possible. Hopefully this will mean that when you relax and breathe out there is some slack in the rope. This will make your wriggle to freedom much easier. If your wrists and ankles are being tied, discreetly hold your arms and legs as far apart as you can while they are being bound.

The rope escape is all about getting a feel for the rope. First wriggle a little and try to feel where the ropes are loosening and try and poke out an elbow or an arm. Once one of your arms is free you can begin to work on the knots with your hand.

If your feet are tied, try to slip off your shoes, as this will make getting free much easier.

THE CAR-BOOT ESCAPE

Car boots are hot and stuffy places, so it is essential to remain calm. Panicking will raise your heart rate, increase your body temperature, which makes the boot hotter, and increase your breathing, which uses up valuable oxygen. Focus your attention on escape and breathe slowly and regularly.

It sounds obvious, but look for a quick-release mechanism. Many new cars have these installed. It would be located near the catch that keeps the boot closed, and rather helpfully, it may even glow in the dark.

If there is no quick release, look for a boot-release cable. Search under the carpet, or along the sides of the boot. When you find the cable, pull it to release the catch.

A car's tail lights can usually be accessed from inside the boot. You might have to remove a panel in the boot to get to them. Once you find the lights, try to push or kick out the unit. This will let in some air and create a space from which you can signal for help to passing cars and pedestrians.

SURVIVAL SKILL WARNING:

A car boot is hot, cramped and almost airtight, so there's not much oxygen on offer and you could suffocate. Do not ever, under any circumstances, shut yourself or anyone else in a car boot.

HOW TO SURVIVE RADIATION

You have been lucky enough to survive a nuclear explosion. You might be tempted to pat yourself on the back for beating the blast, but you're still facing danger. Radioactive dust produced by the blast will settle on the ground. It will remain radioactive for months, even years after the explosion, and will contaminate everything around the bomb site. Radiation can make you extremely sick and will prove fatal in strong doses. To avoid the radiation, you need to get moving and leave the affected area immediately. Travel as far from it as you can.

Spend as little time outside as possible. As you travel away from the affected area, shelter in buildings, preferably those made from concrete. Make your bed for the night as far inside the buildings as possible so that solid materials protect you from the air outside.

Breathing contaminated air is a hazard, but not nearly as dangerous as drinking radiated water or eating contaminated food. Stick to tinned and bottled foods until you have put a lot of distance – and that could mean 200 km – between yourself and the location of the explosion.

Wash thoroughly and regularly with soap and water that has not been contaminated. Drink lots of uncontaminated water to help flush radioactive materials from your system.

HOW TO SURVIVE A SWARM OF ANGRY HONEYBEES

On its own, a honeybee is not particularly dangerous (unless you are allergic to bee stings; if you are, and have been stung, seek immediate medical help). A bee may sting you if it feels threatened, for example if you are about to tread on it. Honeybees die after they sting, so they avoid it if possible. But don't be fooled, those black and yellow stripes mean danger. Bee venom packs a punch, and multiple bee stings are very dangerous and can be fatal.

When bees swarm they can be very aggressive. They want to protect their hive or colony and they are willing to die to do so. Here are some tips about what to do if you encounter a swarm of angry honeybees.

GOOD IDEAS

• Put as much distance as you can between you and the hive. The bees will pursue and sting you until they no longer see you as a threat. Don't stand still, run!

• Take cover, in a building if possible, and shut all the doors and windows. If you can't, run through long grass or scrubland, which should give you some cover.

BAD IDEAS

• Don't approach a hive. Bees are territorial and more likely to attack if you go near their hive.

• Don't swat at the bees. It will make them sting you more as you are threatening their bee buddies.

• Don't attempt to escape by getting into the water. They may wait above the water for you to surface.

DEALING WITH STINGS

A honeybee will leave its stinger in you once it has stung. Gently scrape this out with your fingernail as soon as you can to stop it injecting more venom.

Apply a cold compress to relieve the pain and swelling. Alternatively, apply a substance called 'meat tenderizer' (such as papain) to the area of the sting. This will break down the protein in the bee's venom. A paste of baking soda and water may also soothe the pain.

If you have been unlucky enough to receive more than a dozen stings, or have been stung in or around your mouth or nose, seek medical attention immediately.

HOW TO TICKLE A FISH

Tickling a fish, also known as 'noodling', is an old poachers' trick (a poacher is someone who unlawfully takes or kills fish or game). It is the art of taking a live fish from water with your bare hands. Unsurprisingly, it is illegal, so this is a survival skill that you should only use if you are stranded in the outdoors without any food.

1. Find a stream or river with a good flow of clear water that is no deeper than knee-high.

2. Walk slowly and quietly along the bank upstream (which means in the opposite direction to the current). Keep low, and look out for fish lying close to the bank, near weeds and under stones – in running water, stationary fish always face upstream, so that water can pass through their gills as they open and close their mouths, allowing them to breathe. Concentrate. The fish are not always easy to spot. Stop and crouch down as soon as you see one – you don't want to scare the fish away. Choose a part of the river or stream where the sun isn't behind you, otherwise your shadow will fall on the water and spook any fish.

3. When you've found a fish close enough to your bank, stay just behind it, out of its sight. Then lie on the bank on your belly. Inch forward towards the edge until you are next to the fish, but don't thump on the bank – fish can feel the vibrations through the water.

4. Next, very slowly and gently, so as not to startle your slippery friend, inch your hand and arm into the water until your hand is behind the fish's tail, on the side of the fish away from the bank.

5. Slowly move your hand forward until it is just beneath the fish's gills, and then bring it upwards until you are just touching the fish. Move your hand millimetre by millimetre, and immediately stop and let the fish settle if it shows signs of being disturbed.

6. Now, using a very light touch, slowly move your hand back along the fish's tummy, and continue to repeat this stroking gesture until the fish starts moving its tail and gills in glee and looking like it is mesmerized.

7. Now act with lightning speed. Quickly and firmly close your hand around the fish just behind the gills, and in the same movement flick it out of the water and on to the bank, far enough away from the edge that it can't wriggle back into the stream.

8. Since you want to eat your catch, take a firm hold of it and kill it at once by knocking it sharply on the top of the head – at a point just behind the eyes – with a stone or heavy stick.

9. Find out how to gut the fish for cooking below.

HOW TO GUT A FISH

Preparing a fish you've caught for cooking is very simple. If you do it right, your fish will be safe to eat and free from nasty-tasting body parts that might spoil your feast.

GRIME, GUTS AND GILLS

1. Wash the fish thoroughly in clean, cool running water to get rid of any slime or grit.

2. Gently scrape the blunt side of the knife along the fish from its head to its tail. If the scales spring up, carefully scrape them off, then wash the fish again.

3. With a sharp knife cut off the head behind the gills. Be extremely careful with the knife – you don't want to end up serving real-life 'fish fingers'. Turn the fish right-side up and begin by cutting through the backbone behind the head, and then make the knife cut through the curve of the gill cover until the head is free.

4. Turn the fish on its back and insert the point of the knife into the 'vent' – the small opening on the underside, near the tail. Run the blade up through the skin and thin flesh towards where the head was, opening the fish's body and exposing the insides.

5. Grab a handful of insides at the tail end and pull them out, working towards the head end, until the fish is clear of everything.

6. Carefully use the knife tip to remove the 'kidney line'. This is a dark reddish line that runs along the fish's backbone.

7. Cut off the fins, including, if you want to, the tail. To remove the large fin on the fish's back, insert the knife on one side of the fin and cut the length of the fin. Do the same on the other side, pulling the fin free at the same time.

8. Wash the fish again, both inside and outside to remove any remaining blood, insides or other bits.

Your cleaned fish can now be baked, fried or barbecued on your campfire. If it's big, you can even cut it into seriously delicious steaks.

SURVIVAL SKILL WARNING:

Make sure the fish you've caught is safe to eat. Some fish are poisonous, while others simply taste horrible.

HOW TO GET RID OF LEECHES

The bad news is leeches are blood-sucking, slug-like creatures that lurk in damp places, such as rainforests, tropical jungles, marshes and swamps, just waiting to stick themselves on your skin and gorge themselves on your blood. The good news is that they are not usually harmful, but they can carry bacteria and viruses. So here's how to deal with the little suckers if you need to:

1. In places where leeches are plentiful, if you wade through water they will find you, and if you stand still for a few minutes, you'll see leeches dropping from vegetation and moving towards you. They are attracted by the sound you make and your scent. Use insect repellent on your skin and clothing. Cover as much of your skin as possible. Full armour is an option but you are in danger of sinking in boggy terrain!

2. When on an expedition, regularly check your skin to see if any leeches have attached themselves to you.

3. If you find a leech locate the 'oral' sucker. This is at the thinner end of the leech. Slide a nail sideways underneath and scrape the leech off your skin gradually.

4. When the thin end of the leech has been unstuck, quickly slide your finger under the fat end to dislodge it too. Watch out, the leech will try hard to reattach itself.

5. Carefully check the rest of your body for more leeches. You never know where they could be hiding.

6. Make sure any wounds on your skin caused by leeches stay clean – that way they have less chance of becoming infected.

LEECH DON'TS

• Never be tempted to wrench a leech off your body. Bits of its jaws might get left in your skin and cause an infection.

• Don't try to burn the leech off with a flame or tip salt over it. The leech might let go and fall off, but before it does it might spit the blood that it has sucked out back into your blood along with all sorts of nasty bacteria.

HOW TO PUT SOMEONE IN THE RECOVERY POSITION

If you find a member of your expedition unconscious immediately call for assistance from a qualified medic. If you suspect they have a neck or spine injury, do not attempt to move them unless they are in immediate danger. The recovery position is a first-aid technique that can be used on a teammate who is unconscious, but is still breathing normally and who doesn't have a neck or spinal injury.

Open the patient's mouth and make sure that his airway is clear of any blockages, including his tongue. Tilt his head back and raise his chin. Check that the patient is breathing normally by looking to see if his chest is moving up and down regularly, listening at his mouth and feeling the air on your cheek. Then check that his heart is still beating by feeling for his pulse.

You are now ready to put the patient in the recovery position.

1. Gently lay the patient on his back. Kneel by his right-hand side. Take the arm nearest to you and lay it on the ground in a right angle.

2. Reach over and take the other hand and bring it across his chest. Bend the arm and place the back of the hand on the patient's cheek nearest to you, holding it there with your own hand.

3. Pull up the far (left) leg at his knee until the sole of his foot is on the ground. Then, gently bring the knee towards you (still keeping your hand and the patient's against his cheek). As his left knee comes forward, your casualty should role on to his right side.

4. Remove your hand from the patient's cheek making sure that his head is still resting on his hand. Move the leg towards the chest to form a right angle.

5. Keep the airway open by tilting the patient's head back and raising his chin. Check his breathing and pulse.

6. Keep a close eye on your teammate until help arrives, and check his breathing regularly.

HOW TO BRING AN AIRCRAFT DOWN IN AN EMERGENCY

An indulgent godparent has paid for you to have a two-hour flight in a light aircraft. Forty minutes after taking off, you are cruising at 6,000 feet at a steady 150 mph and enjoying looking at the landscape unfolding beneath you. Suddenly, the pilot suffers a blackout (a sudden case of violent food poisoning) and slumps back in his seat, unconscious. Only you can prevent disaster . . .

1. Don't panic! Many light aircraft have autopilot (a device which, once set and engaged, automatically keeps the plane on a preset course). This will keep the plane flying on the settings the pilot has dialled in. Even if there is no autopilot, the pilot will have 'trimmed' the aircraft to fly 'hands off'. This means that the plane will maintain a steady speed, course and height. Additionally, the pilot will have filed a flight plan, so local air-traffic control (ATC) will be aware of your flight.

2. Make sure the pilot's feet are not obstructing the rudder pedals (these are pretty much where the pedals in a car are). Check that his hands or body are not obstructing the control column or 'yoke' (sometimes called the 'joystick'). Most modern light aircraft have dual controls, so you should be able to land the plane from the co-pilot's seat to the right of the pilot. (If the aircraft has only one set of controls, you will need to drag the pilot out of his seat and take over.)

3. Sit down, but don't touch the controls immediately. On the instrument panel in front of you (usually in the

centre of the top row of instruments in front of the pilot)
there is a device called an 'attitude indicator', also known
as an 'artificial horizon' or 'gyro horizon'. This shows the
position of the aircraft relative to the ground – that is,
whether the wings are level, and whether the aircraft is
climbing or descending, or flying at a steady height. It
shows a pair of straight lines that represent the plane's
wings. Behind them is a sphere or
ball divided horizontally; the
upper half is usually blue
(for sky) and the lower
half usually brown
(for earth).

Check to see if the
two lines on the attitude
indicator representing the
aircraft's wings and the white
dot between them showing the
position of the aircraft's nose line
up with the fixed line on the instrument face representing
the horizon. If they don't, it means the 'autopilot' is off
and the plane is not following a level course.

4. If the autopilot is off, you need to level the plane.
Move the yoke in front of you little by little to get the
wing lines on the attitude indicator level with the line
representing the horizon. Pull the yoke towards you to
bring the nose of the plane up. Push it forward to bring
the nose down. Move the yoke to the left and the plane
will bank left, and to the right it will bank right. Do this
using gentle movements of the yoke, until the plane is
flying straight and level. The attitude indicator will show
the wings horizontal and the nose of the aircraft on the

line between the 'sky' and 'ground' indicators. Do not use the rudder pedals.

5. There is a radio on the instrument panel, probably in the centre. If you can't find a microphone on the instrument panel, take the pilot's headset. Press the PTT (Push To Talk) button and say 'Mayday' three times, clearly and slowly. Then say 'Pilot unconscious'. Release the PTT button so that the person who receives the call can talk back.

6. Below the radio is the 'transponder'. This identifies the aircraft on radar and will send out your location details so your plane can be tracked by ATC. Set the dials to 7700 (or type this number in – it is the code for 'general emergency') and ATC will know you have a problem.

7. The controller will give step-by-step instructions how to land the plane. Follow these carefully, but don't hesitate to ask for things to be repeated if you are at all unsure. Essentially, he will instruct you how to bring the aircraft down to a height from which it can be safely landed. He will tell you what to do about controlling engine power, lowering the undercarriage, and turning on to a new course. He will talk you through the other instruments – such as the altimeter (measures the aircraft's height above the ground) and the airspeed indicator. Everything in flying is geared to height, speed, course, and attitude (the angle relative to the Earth at which the aircraft is flying), and ATC's instructions will aim to keep these four factors correct at any stage during the landing. You might have to land in a field or on a road, so watch out for power lines and trees, or other obstructions, such as bridges.

8. Approach your landing place in a straight line. Just before you reach the ground, pull back slightly on the yoke to lift the nose of the aircraft. This way you'll land on the main wheels beneath the wings – as you slow, the nose wheel will come down.

9. When the plane's main wheels are on the ground, immediately reduce your speed by pulling the throttle (a big black lever between the pilot and co-pilot seats, or a large knob, usually black, in the lower centre of the instrument panel) right back towards you. Many light aircraft have toe brakes on the rudder pedals. If these are fitted, gently press them to bring the plane to a standstill without making it skid.

10. There may be a key, like a car's ignition key, on the instrument panel. Turn this to kill the engine, once the aircraft has come to a halt. Do what you can to help the pilot, but wait until the propeller stops turning before attempting to climb out.

HOW TO SURVIVE AN AVALANCHE

Snow avalanches occur when the snow on a mountain slope becomes so heavy that all it wants to do is travel downhill. Over a million avalanches happen every year, so they're a serious hazard during an expedition in mountains.

AVOID THE DANGER

Always make sure you carry a snow shovel and an avalanche rescue beacon. The beacon will send out a signal that rescuers can follow if you are buried in snow. Turn the beacon on when you set out on your expedition.

Before crossing a slope, secure your snow goggles and put on your hat, gloves and a scarf. Zip up your coat and tighten the neck and cuffs. If an avalanche does happen, it will be harder for the snow to get inside your clothes.

Choose one member of your team to make their way across the slope first. Then make sure everyone in your team crosses in the same track. Tell them to concentrate on the snow on the slope above them for any sign of movement.

AVALANCHE!

Just before an avalanche hits, scream as loud as you can to warn the other members of your team, but when the snow reaches you, close your mouth so you don't swallow any.

Don't try to outrun or out-ski the avalanche – it can move at speeds of over 100 km per hour.

Avalanche snow is a bit like water. Once the snow has hit you and knocked you off your feet, try to swim through the snow. You can stay nearer the surface by swimming upwards, and this improves your chances of being rescued. If you can, grab a tree or a rock to stop yourself sliding down the slope. Failing this, as you come to a halt, curl up in a ball with your hands over your face while the snow covers you. Next, wiggle your head around in the snow to make a breathing space.

If you can see light, try to escape, or at least reach your hand above the surface where it can be seen. Don't waste valuable energy struggling if you aren't getting anywhere. Your avalanche beacon will be sending out signals giving your location, so remain calm and wait for help.

HOW TO SURVIVE IN BEAR COUNTRY

Bears are as reluctant to bump into you as you are to bump into them. Unfortunately, they can't resist the smell of the food you have brought on your expedition. It's essential to do everything you can to avoid bears visiting your camp for lunch.

THE BEAR NECESSITIES

1. Never store food in your tent – keep it at least 50 m from camp in bear-proof boxes. Alternatively, store your food in an airtight container, put it in a bag, and hang it from the branch of a tree. Select a branch strong enough to support the bag but not a bear climbing along it.

2. Establish your cooking area at least 50 m from camp. Always clean up thoroughly after eating. Burn or bury all leftover food well away from camp. Dispose of all cooking or washing-up water away from camp, too.

3. Never keep scented items or toiletries in your tent. Toothpaste and lip-balms are tasty treats for bears.

4. Don't burn 'citronella' candles (sold to keep insects away). Their lemony scent has been known to attract bears.

5. Never put food out for bears in the hope you will spot one. They will only come closer and closer hoping for more food and might get angry when you can't give them any more.

6. When you are out and about, make plenty of noise. Any bears in the area will probably stay out of your way. Attach bells to your ankles or clap and sing as you hike. This is particularly important when other noises, such as rushing water, may hide the sound of your footsteps.

BEAR BEWARE!

• If a bear approaches, don't turn and run or shout and scream. Speak in a calm voice and back away with your head tilted downwards (but keep your eyes on the bear).

• If a bear attacks you play dead. Roll onto your front and curl into a ball clasping your hands behind your neck. Stay in this position until the bear loses interest. It might just be curious and want to play around with you for a bit. If it doesn't show signs of leaving you alone, or becomes more ferocious, fight it off with all your might.

HOW TO BUILD A SURVIVAL SHELTER

This easy survival shelter can be made in a couple of hours. It will keep you warm and dry, and will help you get a good night's sleep, which is vital in preserving your strength and maintaining a positive attitude. Here's how to build it:

1. Find two strong, straight sticks, each with a fork at one end. Make sure they are the same length (about 1.2 m). Sharpen the unforked ends and dig them firmly into the ground to a depth of at least 40 cm, and 2 m apart. If one stick is longer than the other, dig it further into the ground to even up the height.

2. Find another long, straight stick over 2 m long and rest this in the forks of the upright sticks. This is your 'ridge pole'. Secure it to the forked sticks with twine.

3. If you have a tarpaulin throw it over the ridge pole to make a tent. If it is large enough, use some of the tarpaulin to form a floor for you to make your bed on.

4. Peg the tarpaulin down with sticks, or place heavy stones along the wall edges to keep it secure.

AN ALTERNATIVE SHELTER

If you don't have a tarpaulin, make a shelter by building two walls out of branches and poles.

1. Find a long pole (about one and a half times as high as the tallest person using the shelter). Find a tree with a forked branch to support your shelter at one end.

2. Place the pole against the tree, then place smaller poles each side of the main pole to make a sloping framework. Next, weave some thin, bendy branches through the small poles to make a criss-cross frame.

3. Cover your frame with materials such as dead leaves, dry ferns, moss and grass. Add some light branches to the outside of the shelter to stop your insulating material blowing away. Then spread a thick layer of dry grass on the floor of the shelter for you to lie on.

HOW TO SURVIVE A VISIT FROM AN ABOMINABLE SNOWMAN

Picture yourself trekking through the Himalayas in Tibet. There are many dangers you will have prepared for before setting out – the cold, snowy conditions, the treacherous, rocky landscape, the low oxygen levels that you will find at this high altitude. What you might have forgotten to prepare for, however, is a visit from an abominable snowman, known to his friends as a 'yeti'.

Some people don't actually believe that yetis exist, but just in case you encounter one here are some rules to follow:

1. Never enter into a long discussion with him or her about whether or not you believe in yetis. This is guaranteed to make a yeti very angry. Imagine if you had trekked across a wild and desolate landscape in search of food or company only to be told that you don't exist. Wouldn't that make you abominably bad-tempered?

2. Don't run around screaming or throwing things at the yeti. Yetis are bigger and stronger than you and if you make them cross they may attack. Stay calm and slowly back away with your arms out in front of you, your hands clearly visible and palms downwards. This will put the yeti at ease and show him that you are not about to reach for something to throw at him.

3. Some people believe yetis are the distant cousins of human beings. So why not offer the yeti a cup of tea

66

or some food? Snow people are often amazed by our abominable lack of manners when receiving guests. When a yeti has guests they will always offer some wild rhododendron tea and a few snow biscuits at the very least, even if the guest was not invited.

4. Don't flash cameras in a yeti's face – snow people find this very rude. Always ask the yeti's permission before taking their photograph so they have enough time to arrange their fur in a pleasing way. If you ask the yeti nicely enough they may even let you pose in the shot with them.

HOW TO TIE
A QUICK-RELEASE KNOT

This quick-release knot is ideal for tying up something just for a little while, such as a hammock that you want to have a quick nap in. The knot will stay put, but if you tug on the loose end you can make it unravel.

1. Put a loop round a post or tree.

2. Make a kink and pass it through your loop.

3. Make another kink from the lower end of the rope.

4. Pass this kink through the first kink. Pull on the long end of the rope to secure the knot.

5. To release the knot, pull on the short end.

HOW TO SEND AN SOS

If you find yourself in need of rescuing, whether stranded on land or at sea, your priority is to attract the attention of potential rescuers. You need to send out an urgent signal for help called an 'SOS'. Here are some ways to do this.

FIRE, FIRE!

Fires are effective if they are built in a clearing. By day, the smoke can be seen for miles. By night, the light from a fire will be visible from even further away. Three fires arranged in the shape of a triangle is a well-known distress signal. Add leaves, fresh grass, ferns and damp wood to your fires to produce smoke, which will increase visibility during daylight. Use drier wood for a brighter blaze at night-time.

- Make sure there is nothing near by that can catch light if your signal fires flare up or blow out sparks, and don't build any fires in a dry or wooded area.

• Never signal for help unless you genuinely need it – you might spark a false rescue attempt.

• When you have finished signalling remember to put out your signal fires by covering them with soil or pouring water on them until all the embers have stopped glowing.

GOT THE MESSAGE?

'Morse code' uses a combination of long and short pulses of light or sound to communicate letters and numbers. An SOS in Morse code can be sent using a torch. Alternatively use a shiny surface, such as a mirror or a polished piece of metal, to reflect sunlight. Direct your flashes of light towards the ship or aircraft you are trying to attract.

To send an SOS in Morse code, repeat this sequence: three short flashes, three longer flashes, three short flashes.

PLANE SPOTTER

To make sure you alert a passing helicopter or plane to your location, mark out a large signal on the ground that can be seen from the air. Reflective materials, such as metal wreckage from a car or plane, or any brightly coloured materials, are ideal. Use branches or stones if that's all you can find. Arrange the objects so they spell out 'SOS', or form a geometric shape, such as a triangle or square. In nature objects rarely form regular shapes – a search party is much more likely to notice an unnatural, man-made arrangement of objects.

• Stop signalling if you are certain that your signal has been seen – otherwise you might confuse your original SOS or dazzle the pilot of an aircraft.

• When you are rescued, make sure any SOS signals that you have made on the ground are cleared away. That way nobody else will see them and think someone needs help.

HOW TO SURVIVE A ZOMBIE INVASION

A zombie attack is probably the hardest challenge you will face. Zombies (or the 'undead', as they prefer to be known) are notoriously difficult to kill because they are not actually alive. As soon as you hear reports of zombies in your area, follow this plan of action.

GAME PLAN

Gather as many survivors of the invasion as you can – there is safety in numbers. Find yourselves a secure building to use as a base. Ideally it should be on high ground. This will offer an excellent vantage point from which you can spot zombie hordes approaching, and the undead can't climb because their knees don't bend. Stock plenty of food and water – you may be surrounded by the undead for days.

Make sure the building has only two entrances (you need a second exit to escape through if zombies break through the front entrance). Build a barricade at each entrance and seal any other doors and windows with heavy furniture.

HOW TO SPOT A ZOMBIE

The living dead are easy to spot because, as their name suggests, they are dead people whose bodies have come alive again. Look out for staring eyes, green skin and a pungent smell of rotting and decay. Check for a distinctive way of walking – slowly stumbling, with arms held straight out in front and a limp caused by their stiff knees.

If survivors come to your base asking for shelter – beware. They may have been infected. This happens if they are bitten or scratched by a zombie. There is no cure. They will become zombies too. Check all newcomers for any wounds.

If someone has been infected you must get them out of your safe house quickly. The good news is once they are a full-blown zombie they won't feel pain and they'll never be forced to do anything they don't want to again, such as be nice to their granny. The bad news is they'll stink and their flesh will fall off.

BATTLING WITH THE UNDEAD

After a while you may get bored of waiting it out in barricaded base. Television broadcasts will eventually stop and there'll be nothing but the sound of static on the radio. You may decide to venture outside. Be very careful. Whenever you leave the shelter to gather fresh supplies or check for more survivors, carry a bat or sword to defend yourself. Guns are useless against zombies. You can knock a zombie's head off though, and stop it in its tracks.

If you find yourself caught in a crowd of the undead, your best chance of surviving is to act like a zombie. Moan and keep your eyes as wide open as possible. Limp and dribble. Zombies are pretty stupid and with any luck they won't notice you among them.

HOW TO ESCAPE FROM QUICKSAND

Quicksand is a thick sludge that is most commonly found near beaches or rivers. In the movies people slowly sink into it, unable to escape, until their heads finally disappear beneath the surface and they're never seen again.

In reality, getting stuck in quicksand doesn't mean an inevitable death. It is often only a couple of feet deep and you'll stop sinking when your feet touch the solid bottom.

BE PREPARED

Most people who perish in quicksand die by drowning. This is because quicksand is usually found in tidal areas. When the tide comes in the area is submerged under water, as is anyone stuck in the sand. The most important thing thing is to be prepared and not to allow yourself to get stuck.

- If you are travelling in a team, spread out. Make sure you walk with a ten-pace gap between each team member. This way if one of you starts sinking the others can stop and help rather than take a mud bath with you.

- Use a stick to prod and test the ground in front of you.

- Carry a length of rope that you can use to lasso near by objects and pull yourself clear in emergencies.

- Walk barefoot. The soles of shoes can act like a sink plunger, and will suck you down as you try to pull your feet out quicksand.

ESCAPING A STICKY SITUATION

As soon as you feel you are sinking, throw away any heavy objects you are carrying, such as your rucksack or daypack. You must avoid allowing your feet to plunge down into the sand under the weight of your body. Quickly lean your whole body backwards until you are lying flat. This will spread out your weight and help you float on the surface of the sand. Breathe in deeply and fill your lungs with air to increase your buoyancy.

Lie still. Don't thrash around. Any sudden movements will stir up the quicksand and make it less stable. Wait for the sand to settle around you. Carefully manoeuvre your walking stick underneath your hips, so you are lying across it. It will help keep you on the surface.

Stay on your back, but use your arms and legs to swim, crawl and drag yourself towards solid terrain. Move very slowly, inching your way to firmer ground.

HOW TO TRACK
A WILD ANIMAL

Before you can track down a wild animal, you must be able to recognize its footprints. Memorize the animal tracks below, then read on for how to find your beast.

Here are some tracks you won't mind finding:

dog   cat   fox   badger   running rabbit

Here are some tracks you should not follow:

hyena   bear   hippo   mountain lion

TRACKER TIPS

• The best time to go tracking is early in the morning or late in the day. When the sun is low in the sky, tracks will be edged with shadow, making them more visible.

- Always take a tracking guidebook with you, so you can identify any unusual tracks you come across.

- Scout around for tracks. Brush loose leaves and vegetation aside. Keep an eye out for animal trails. These are routes that animals take regularly where soil and vegetation will appear to be worn down.

- When you find a trail of prints, mark each one by pushing a stick into the ground next to it. This will help you to see the animal's stride pattern. From this you will be able to speculate on the size and type of animal you are tracking.

- Use a magnifying glass to look closely at the prints. You might find an animal has a clipped hoof or damaged claw that makes its track unique. This will help you distinguish your animal's track from that of other, similar animals.

- Look out for droppings, chewed plants and any other signs of the animal's activity. This will help you identify the animal you are following. The droppings, for example, might have a distinctive smell.

- Don't look down at your feet. You'll track down the animal much faster if you look between 5 m and 10 m away from your body.

- Stay low, move slowly and be as quiet as you can. Even the sound of a snapping twig could make your animal run off.

ON THE RIGHT TRACK

As you get closer to the animal you are tracking, its footprints will become cleaner, with less spare dirt, twigs and leaves lying on top of them. Its droppings, being fresher, will be warmer and softer. At this point, slow down in case you come across the animal and startle it.

If you need to hide, take refuge in a bush and get down on your hands and knees – failing that, lie down in some long grass and inch along the ground using your arms.

If the wind is behind you, you might want to leave the trail and creep around the outside of the animal's tracks, so that your scent doesn't get blown towards the animal and scare it away.

HOW TO MAKE A TRACKING STICK

Animal tracking is great fun, and this tracking stick will help you master the art.

1. Find a branch about a metre in length.

2. Use this to measure the distance between one footprint and the next footprint left by the same foot, from heel to heel. This will give you the length of the animal's stride. Use a sharp stone to scratch a mark on your stick in the position of each heel (X and Z).

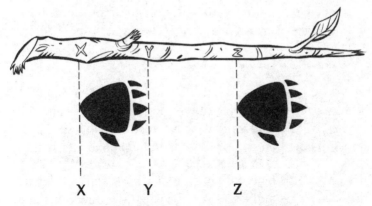

X   Y   Z

3. Hold the stick with point X at the heel of the first footprint and measure the length of this print. Use your stone to mark the front of the print as point Y.

4. To begin using the stick, hold it so that point X is over the heel of the rearmost print and then look close to point Z for the next track. Repeat this process until you track down your animal.

HOW TO STAGE A JAILBREAK

You are in a faraway country and find yourself imprisoned (obviously due to an unfortunate misunderstanding and through absolutely no mistake of your own) in a lonely prison cell. Don't despair – start planning your escape.

THE BREAK-THROUGH

Brick walls are among the easiest walls to escape through:

1. Scrape out the mortar around a single brick using a key, a spoon or any sharp object. This will take days. When you're not working on the brick, mix the scraped-out mortar with water or spit and push it back into place. This will make the brick look untouched.

THE BOYS' BOOK OF SURVIVAL

Choose a brick that is hidden from view by your bed or a piece of furniture, and make sure you cover it up after every scraping session.

2. Once one brick is out, the bricks around it will be a lot easier to remove. Only take out the minimum number of bricks you need to form a hole through which you can squeeze.

3. When it comes to the actual escape, you need to pick your moment. You need to work out your guards' routine. They will check your cell at regular intervals. You need to time your escape immediately after they have visited, thus giving you the maximum time to get away before they check your cell again. The best time is at night, because the number of guards patrolling outside your cell will be at a minimum and your movements will be under the cover of darkness. When you are ready to go, make it look like you are still in your bed by putting pillows or spare clothes under your blanket. With a bit of luck the guards might not know you've escaped until morning. By then you'll be long gone.

4. As you leave your cell, reach back through the hole and pull the furniture back in front of it, so that it can't be easily seen from your cell door.

SURVIVAL SKILL WARNING:

Don't ever try to escape through your bedroom wall. Your room will get a bit draughty and someone's bound to spot the hole sooner or later.

HOW TO MAKE A GETAWAY

You are on the run and need to put as much distance between yourself and your pursuers as possible. Here's how:

DISGUISE YOUR TRACKS

Try not to leave an obvious trail. Stick to roads, rocks and other hard surfaces where you won't leave noticeable footprints. If you can't avoid leaving prints, don't waste a lot of time brushing them away. It is essential to move quickly, and brush marks are easy to spot.

'Backtracking' (walking backwards in your own tracks) is an excellent way to confuse trackers:

1. Find a starting spot that will make your trail harder to follow – such as a slab of stone or some shallow water.

2. Walk up to this spot, then walk backwards in your own tracks for ten paces.

3. Leap sideways off your trail and set off in a completely different direction. If the start of your new trail is hidden by a tree or bush, so much the better.

ON THE SCENT

If your pursuers are using tracker dogs, your chances of a clean getaway are smaller unless you can throw the dogs off your scent.

• Scramble over fences or walls which will be hard for the dogs to scale.

- Whenever possible stay downwind of the dogs so they can't pick up your scent on the air.

- Wade through water at every opportunity. This is the most effective way to leave no tracks and no scent.

- If you come to a stream, don't go straight across; if you have time, walk or swim up or down stream for a good distance before getting out on the other bank.

- Whenever possible, mingle with other people in a crowded place, so that your scent will be mixed with the scent of others.

- Best of all, if you can get yourself on a horse or a bicycle you will break your trail, and it will be very difficult for the nosy mutts to sniff you out.

HOW TO SURVIVE AT THE SCHOOL DISCO

Picture the scene – something terrible is playing on the sound system, lights are flashing, your teachers are desperately trying to look cool, and there are girls everywhere. Girls who want to dance with you.

If this situation is right up your street, select the girl you want to dance with. Ask her confidently but nicely to dance. Whisk her onto the dance floor. Whirl her around (roughly in time to the music will do) and throw some serious shapes.

THINGS TO SAY

- 'Do you do modelling for extra cash?' • 'Do you dance professionally?' • 'That colour really suits you.'

THINGS NOT TO SAY

• *'What's that in your hair?'* • *'Where's that smell coming from?'* • *'My friends dared me to ask you to dance.'*

EVASIVE ACTION

If the very thought of girls or dancing sends shivers down your spine, you have two options. You can stay at home, watch TV, feed your goldfish and go to bed early. Alternatively, go to the disco, but bandage one leg or one arm heavily. Stand at the side of the room and look as though you would love to dance, but you simply can't.

Top Tip: If you'd rather dance by yourself you'll need a strategy to keep the girls at a distance. Fling your arms around wildly, get really into the music and sing along loudly. You'll find a wide circle opening up around you.

HOW TO MAKE A CATAPULT

Catapults are great for firing small stones at tin cans in your back garden or for scaring off ferocious animals that may attack your camp in the wilderness. Who knows, your handy little sling could even come in useful for fending off invading aliens or zombies.

CATAPULT CONSTRUCTION

1. Find a strong, but flexible, forked branch (about 2.5 cm thick). An evenly Y-shaped branch works best.

2. Next you need some elastic. Pull a bit out of some old trousers – just be certain you don't want to wear them again. Alternatively, use a bit of the inner tube of a bike's tyre. This will be stronger and less likely to snap.

3. Find a strong, oblong piece of fabric, big enough to hold a large marshmallow. Leather or denim will work well. Thread your elastic through two holes in the fabric so that the pouch sits in the middle as shown below.

4. Tie an end of the elastic sling to each prong of your forked stick.

5. Hold your finished catapult at the base and place a small stone, a conker or a marshmallow in the fabric pouch.

6. Pull back on the sling until the elastic is fully stretched. Aim through the V made by the two upper arms of the catapult. Then let go of the sling to fire the catapult.

You'll need to practise if you want to hit a tin can.

SURVIVAL SKILL WARNING:

Never fire your catapult at a human being.
They certainly won't thank you for it and there's
a serious risk of hurting them.

HOW TO SURVIVE A HUGE SPOT

Have you ever woken up to find a giant spot the size of a volcano taking over your face? You don't have to barricade yourself in your room for days. Deal with it.

• Be realistic. Your zit really won't look as big to anyone else as it does to you. Your friends might not even notice it.

• To prevent the spot from getting infected and swollen, don't rub, squeeze or pick at it as this will just make it red and angry.

• Dab your spot with medicated spot cream or a little diluted tea tree oil.

• There are lots of other ways to banish spots. There are weird remedies, such as washing your face in rose water at full moon while you stand on your head. Feel free to try this if you want to. Rose water might not make any difference to your spots whatsoever, but your granny will think you smell lovely.

• To prevent more spots, make sure you drink plenty of water and eat at least five portions of fresh fruit and vegetables a day (seriously important for anyone hoping to survive).

• Keep your skin clean – wash your face with a gently medicated facewash every day and pat it dry with a clean, soft towel.

HOW TO CARRY SOMEONE TO SAFETY

If someone in your expedition team has sprained their ankle but is still conscious and can hold themselves upright, you can make a stable seat with your hands simply by joining forces with another person.

1. Following the picture shown above, place your right hand on your left wrist, and grip tightly. Ask your lifting partner to do the same.

2. Now grip their right wrist with your left hand and get them to grip your right wrist. (Follow the picture shown on the opposite page.)

3. Lower the seat by both of you bending your legs, not your backs.

4. Get your casualty to sit on the four-handed seat and place his or her arms around both of the lifters' shoulders tightly.

5. When the casualty is seated, stand up, making sure you keep your back straight.

6. As soon as you have carried your casualty to safety find a trained medical person who can examine them.

SAFETY POINTS

- Do not lift anyone that may have a serious injury unless it is absolutely necessary. For example, if they face oncoming danger, such as a fire.

- Always ask someone else for help when lifting. Don't try to lift a casualty on your own or you could end up dropping them and doing them more damage.

HOW TO MAKE AN UNDERWATER ESCAPE

You are deep in the mountains on a road trip, when suddenly the biggest, grizzliest bear lumbers in front of your windscreen. Your car swerves to avoid it and veers off the road, plunging into a near by lake.

You are not doomed. Most cars will float for a while, giving you time to save the day. Immediately remove your seatbelt so you are ready for action.

As soon as your car enters the water, release the door locks. If you can, open the doors before the car begins to sink and use them to escape. You won't be able to open the doors once the car is partially submerged, because the weight of the water is pushing against them.

If the doors won't open, wind down your windows as quickly as possible. Electric windows should still work while your car is afloat, but will stop working as soon as the mechanism or the car's battery is submerged. Climb out of a window and swim to safety.

If you are unable to open your doors or windows, try to smash a window. Use something heavy like a wrench, or the metal end of a headrest. Smash it at the corner as this is where the window is weakest.

If the car sinks before you can do any of the above, you are going to have to wait until the car has filled with water. This will equalize the pressure of the water inside and outside the car. Climb into the back seat because the front of the car, where the heavy engine is, will sink first. Wait until the water has reached neck height. Then instruct everyone to take a big gulp of air. Once the doors are completely submerged, they should open with a push. Try shoving a door with your feet while steadying yourself by grabbing onto a seat. Exit the car, and swim away and up to the surface.

SURVIVAL SKILL WARNING:

Don't ever deliberately fill a car with water.
You might drown accidentally and you certainly
won't be able to ride to the cinema in it.

HOW TO SURVIVE THE BUBONIC PLAGUE

In the unlikely event that you wake up in medieval or Elizabethan England, and discover that an epidemic of the bubonic plague has reached your town or village, here are some tips on how to survive it.

SURVIVAL STRATEGIES

• Symptoms of the plague include a headache, aching joints, a fever and vomiting. Large lumps will appear around your armpits, neck and groin area, and black spots appearing on your skin. These are the 'buboes' from which the plauge takes its name. Watch out for these symptoms in yourself and your family.

• Keep your house clean. By dropping food crumbs on the floor of your kitchen you may attract rats with fleas that are carrying the bubonic plague.

• Don't copy your ancestors and carry flowers around with you because you think they will stop you getting the plague. They might cover up the smell of rotting plague victims, but they certainly won't stop you catching the dreaded disease.

COPING WITH THE CONTAGION

• Shut yourself away in your house, but get word to anyone who has been near you that you have the plague, so they can get some medical help.

• Do not stop bathing. It is essential that you keep your sores really clean so they are less likely to become infected.

• Paint a red cross on your door. This will tell your friends that your household has become infected with the plague and they will know not to visit you after school.

• Alternatively, you could try and survive until the 20th century when antibiotics will be available and your chances of survival will be much greater.

HOW TO SURVIVE A SHOPPING EXPEDITION

It is a bright sunny holiday morning and you are looking forward to getting out to the park with your friends. You go into the kitchen for your breakfast when Mum drops a bombshell: *'I think we should go out to get you some new clothes for school.'*

AARRGGH! This is not what you planned for your day – but don't despair, follow these tips and you could be in the park before lunchtime.

Shopping is like any other expedition and careful planning will help you avoid disaster. Establish a clear objective – what are you going for and where are you going to go for it? This is essential to avoid wandering around shops that don't even sell the things you need.

Establish how long you are going to be out. If your parent is vague on this, beware – they could be planning a whole-day trip. Think of reasons why the trip should be brief.

> *'You said you were going to call so and so . . .'*
> *'Your friend from aerobics said she might pop in after lunch . . .'*
> *'That film you wanted to watch is on this afternoon . . .'*

Get yourself ready quickly, and then get any younger brothers or sisters that are coming with you ready. It's true to say the sooner you head out the sooner you will be back. If you set out early in the morning, you will miss the traffic and the shops will be empty with no queues.

Decide how important a day at the park is to you. Think about this very carefully. Are you are prepared to wear flared trousers three sizes too big and a giant itchy jumper that 'you will grow into' to school every day for the next two years, just to get out to the park? If so, agree to everything your mum wants to buy and you will be there in no time. She may even drop you off.

HOW TO AVOID A HUNGRY HIPPO

You're on an African safari when, out of nowhere, a 2-tonne hungry hippo appears. Hippos can spend up to 16 hours a day chilling out in water, but don't be fooled. They are extremely aggressive, fiercely territorial and very fast. A hippo can run at speeds of up to 48 kilometres an hour and can do so for over 100 metres before it needs to rest.

In short, there's not a great deal you can do to defend yourself against a hippo attack, so your best policy is to avoid one.

- If you encounter a hippo on dry land, don't startle it, walk away as quietly and quickly as possible.

- Never get between a mother hippo and her baby. Female hippos are extremely protective of their young.

- Don't sail down an African river where hippos can be found. Hippos attack people who disturb them when they are having a soak. They can hold their breath under water for five minutes, so just because you can't see a hippo, it doesn't mean that the coast is clear.

- Never jump in the water to swim with a hippo. Bathing like a hippo might look like fun, but you aren't a hippo and there's no way you'll fool the hippo into thinking that you are – no matter how good you are at holding your breath.

HOW TO TIE A SLING

1. Find a large piece of clean fabric, about a metre square. A pillowcase cut open into a square is ideal. Fold the fabric in half diagonally to make a triangle-shaped bandage.

2. Hold the bandage under the casualty's injured arm, placing one end over the opposite shoulder.

3. Bring the other end of the bandage up over the arm, and over the other shoulder.

4. Tie the two ends together at the back of the casualty's neck, making sure the arm is held gently but securely in place.

5. Use a safety pin to fasten the remaining corner of the bandage. Pin the corner to the sling near the elbow.

Top Tip: If you can't find a piece of material to make your sling, try using a piece of clothing such as a jumper.

You might need to practise tying your sling a few times before you get it right, so find a willing friend – if they can sit still long enough.

HOW TO SURVIVE AN ESSAY CRISIS

Help! Your essay is due in the morning and you have been playing computer games all evening. Here's how to save your skin by whipping up an excellent essay in no time.

1. Think carefully about what you want to say. Scribble down some ideas to make a spider diagram. Then join up any ideas that are linked.

2. Organize your ideas on a big piece of paper. If you are presenting some information, divide it into categories. For example, if your subject is the history of exploration, you could have 'The First Explorers', 'Exploration Today' and 'What Is There Left To Discover?' Jot them down as headings, leaving plenty of space between them.

3. List the main points that should go under each heading. List next to each point any facts that back it up.

4. Write an introduction. It might seem odd not to start by writing an introduction, but now is a good time because you know what is in the essay. Just give a brief summary of your essay – don't explain what you have found out though – that's the job of the conclusion.

5. Write your conclusion last. If you have presented an argument (such as 'Why I should lead a team to the North Pole'), round it off by summarizing the main points of the argument that you have already mentioned. For example: 'I would be the youngest explorer to make the journey. As a result people would give me lots of money to finance the trip. I would look really cool in the newspapers pictured standing at the Pole.'

6. Hand in your essay with a proud grin and wait for your teacher to give you top marks.

HOW TO SURVIVE BEING STUCK IN A LIFT

If you find yourself stuck in a lift, remain calm. You are not in a movie and a modern lift is very unlikely to come crashing down (even if the cables snap). Another thing modern lifts don't have is hatches in the ceiling through which you can escape. This would be pretty dumb and dangerous anyway.

Press each of the floor buttons one by one. Then try the 'door open' button. If none of these buttons works the lift is broken and you need to let someone know about it.

If you can see light through any gap between the lift doors, the lift has probably stopped near a floor and it should be easy for you to shout for help and be released. The doors can be opened with a key. Don't try to force the doors open yourself. If the lift starts working when you are halfway out, you could be in for a nasty surprise.

If you can't see light through the doors, you have probably stopped between floors. Look for an emergency telephone. If there isn't one look for an alarm button. Press this repeatedly. Someone should hear you and get help.

If you have waited for more than half an hour and nobody has arrived to help, shout and bang the inside walls of the lift with a set of keys or a shoe. If there are still people in the building, you need to get their help before they leave for the night.

If everyone has left the building and nobody is responding to the alarm, the worst-case scenario is that you could be in the lift overnight. If this happens, there's no point panicking. Make yourself comfortable and get some sleep (and hope you don't need the loo).

HOW TO SURVIVE A SNAKE BITE

Not all snakes are poisonous and even poisonous snakes don't always inject venom into a victim when they bite. However, always assume a snake is poisonous, just in case.

In the movies, the hero usually cuts across their buddy's snake bite with a knife and sucks out the poison. Don't do this. You might make yourself sick, and cutting the flesh around the bite might help the venom to spread and could cause infection.

Get to a hospital as fast as you can. Even if you don't immediately feel unwell, it is essential that you get medical treatment as quickly as possible. If the bite starts to swell up and changes colour, it means the snake that bit you was probably poisonous.

Make a note of the exact time of the bite and of the size and appearance of the snake. This information will help the doctors who treat the bite. If possible, telephone the hospital with these details before you get there – that way they can have the correct treatment ready when you arrive.

SELF-TREATMENT

If you can't get medical attention immediately, remain calm. Panicking will increase your heart rate and this will help the venom spread throughout your body faster.

Take the following precautions:

- If you've been bitten on your arm or hand, remove your watch as your hand or wrist might swell up and your

watch could become painfully stuck. Remove any
other pieces of tight clothing that are near the bite.

• Dress the wound with a bandage that fits snugly,
but not too tightly. You want to restrict the flow of blood
slightly to the bitten area, but not cut off the blood
supply altogether.

• If you're with another member of your expedition party
get them to wash your bite with soap and water. Lie down
flat so that the area of your body that was bitten is not
higher than your heart. This will slow down the speed at
which venom travels to this vital part of your body. Tell
them to tie a splint to the affected limb. This will restrict
its movement and help prevent the venom from moving
around the body.

HOW TO AVOID
A MAN-EATING TIGER

Tigers usually don't attack and eat humans unless they are old or injured and unable to hunt for other food. However, in some rare cases, a single tiger that has turned into a 'man-eater' has been know to kill dozens or even hundreds of people.

TIGER TIPS

You find out that a man-eating tiger is on the loose in your vicinity, and may find its way to your camp, town or village. Here's how to prepare for and deal with the danger:

1. Make a papier-mâché face mask. Wear it on the back of your head, not your face, so you look as if you have two faces – one at the front and one at the back. A tiger doesn't like to jump on its prey from the front and your mask will confuse it.

2. Carry a club over your right shoulder at all times. Tigers attack humans on the back of their neck so you will be ready to defend yourself.

3. If you catch sight of the tiger just before it pounces, turn to face it and look it right in the eye.

4. If you see the tiger in the distance, make a run for it. Tigers won't try and chase you over long distances. If a tiger thinks you have already seen it and you are quite far away, it might just leave you alone and wait and for another piece of meat to come along.

Top Tip: Don't bother leaping into the village pond local pool and don't climb a tree or scramble on top of a bus shelter. Tigers are excellent swimmers and climbers so it will soon catch up with you.

HOW TO PREDICT RAIN

Knowing whether or not it is going to rain is an invaluable skill when leading an expedition. Rain can make surfaces dangerous and your team's progress slow, plus your friends will appreciate staying dry!

Sometimes all you need to do is take a quick look at your teammates' hair to judge whether the weather is about to change. This is because some curly-headed folk will find their hair curls up more tightly before it rains.

Alternatively, most flowers are quick to open up when rain threatens. Regularly check the air to tell if the scent of any near by blooms has become noticeably stronger.

Stay alert to unusual animal behaviour, too. Animals are often aware of differences in air pressure, which indicate a change in the weather. If you notice that buzzing insects have suddenly gone quiet or that birds have returned to the trees, it's probably a sign that you're about to get drenched and it's time for you to seek shelter as well.

CLOUD READING

Grey clouds in the sky don't necessarily mean that a heavy shower is brewing, but the skies can give you essential information about the weather. Check the following:

Time of day. A grey morning sky can actually be a sign of a glorious day to come, but if the sky turns grey and clouds over later in the afternoon it means rain is probable.

Shape. Thin and wispy clouds that are spaced far apart signal fine weather. When they gather together and get ominously larger, they are likely to produce rain quite suddenly.

Height. As a general rule, the higher a cloud is in the sky, the better the weather will be. A covering of low, dark cloud is usually bad news, suggesting a lengthy downpour is probably on the way.

Colour. Clouds that are dark underneath and very tall usually mean that thunder, lightning, hail and strong winds are plotting to wreak havoc.

HOW TO BUILD AN IGLOO

1. Use a stick to mark a circle in the snow about 3.5 m across. Grab a snow shovel and dig out the circle to a depth of about 15 cm. Trample down the circle of snow with your feet.

2. Find a large, clear area of deep snow near by and jump on it until it is flat. This is going to be your snow quarry.

3. Use your shovel to cut out some snow bricks about 70 cm long, 50 cm wide and 20 cm deep.

4. Build a layer of snow bricks around the outside of your circle. Shape the bricks so that the row makes a spiral shape. (Leave a gap for the entrance.) Get a friend to work from the inside of the igloo, filling in the cracks with snow.

5. Build a second layer of bricks, cutting each brick so that they continue to make a spiral. Then create more layers of bricks until you have an igloo shape with a hole at the top.

6. 'Cap' the hole with a single block of packed snow. Cut a block that is slightly bigger than the hole and get your partner to help lift it up and put it in place.

7. Climb inside the igloo and trim the cap so that it fits the hole. Pack snow around the edges of the cap.

8. Dig out a little trench from the snow leading up to the entrance hole.

9. Make an arch over your entrance hole by placing two narrow bricks either side. Make sure the arch will be big enough for you to crawl through easily.

10. Make a couple of small slits near the top and bottom of the igloo. These will allow air in and out.

SURVIVAL SKILL WARNING:

Keep your igloo-building skills for Arctic expeditions. Igloos can be dangerous if they collapse on top of you. So at home, stick to snuggling up in your own heated home. And if you must build an igloo in snowy territory, make sure you don't do it alone.

HOW TO MAKE FRESH WATER FROM SEA WATER

If you are marooned on a desert island after a shipwreck, you'll be surrounded by water. Annoyingly, you won't be able to drink any of it because it is salty. With any luck, you'll have salvaged some useful utensils, such as cooking pots and tin cans, from the wreck of the ship. Using these, here's how to make delicious fresh water from nasty brine.

1. Stand a clean, empty tin can on the bottom of an empty cooking pot or bowl. Pop a stone into the can to keep it in place.

2. Pour seawater into the pot until the level is about three quarters the height of the can. Make sure the seawater does not enter the can.

3. Put the pot's lid on upside-down, so that the lid handle is over the empty can inside. Put the pot over a campfire and wait for the water to boil.

4. As the water boils, carefully pour a little cold seawater over the lid of the pot to keep it cool. Make sure that your fire doesn't go out. As the water boils it turns to steam and leaves the salt particles behind in the pan. The steam collects on the inside of the lid and, as it cools, 'condenses' into pure water droplets. The condensation then runs down the lid's handle, dripping into the can. Keeping the outside of the lid cool with cold water makes the steam condense faster.

5. After 20 minutes use some twigs as tongs to lift the lid of the pot and check the water's progress. Once the can is almost full, very carefully remove it from the pot with the tongs. The pot, can and water will be very hot.

6. Leave the can of water to cool before drinking.

SURVIVAL SKILL WARNING:

Don't try doing this unless you have been shipwrecked. Seawater tastes disgusting and is extremely bad for you if it has not been boiled in the correct way because it contains huge amounts of salt.

HOW TO LIGHT A FIRE

There are a several ways of making fire if you don't have any matches or a lighter. The 'fire-bow drill' is a clever version of the 'rubbing two sticks together' method. Here's how to do it:

1. Collect some 'tinder'. Tinder is anything that catches fire very easily, such as dry, thin grass, cotton fluff and feathers. You need a good handful to start your fire.

2. Find a wooden stick for your bow. It needs to be a strong stick that is about 60 cm long and about 1 cm wide. It must be quite stiff, but still bendable. A thin bamboo cane is good for this.

3. Now you need some cord or string. A bootlace is perfect if it is long enough. Carefully carve a slight notch around each end of the bow. Attach the cord to the bow at either end around the notches. The cord should be stretched tightly enough to make the bow bend slightly.

4. The drill should be a piece of hard, dry branch about 30 cm long and 2.5 cm wide. It should have a sharp point at one end and be rounded and blunt at the other. The straighter your drill, the easier it will be to use. Twist the drill into your cord (see the picture opposite).

5. Make a base called a 'fireboard'. You will need a flat piece of soft, dry wood, 2.5 cm thick, 15 cm wide and 60 cm long.

6. Carve a v-shaped notch in one end of the board about 2 cm deep and 2 cm wide, as shown below. Put your tinder in the notch.

7. Make a hole in the board that is about the same width as your drill and 1.5 cm deep. The hole should be centred near the notch you made.

8. Find a stone with a natural hollow in it, about the same size as the blunt end of your fire drill. Push the blunt end of your drill in the stone's hollow and rest the sharp end in the hole on your board. Alternatively, make a hole in a piece of hardwood that fits in your hand and use that instead of the stone.

9. Kneel on one knee and place your other foot firmly on the fireboard. Push down lightly on the stone with one hand and hold the bow in your other. Pull the bow back forth. Begin slowly, and keep a steady pace.

Spin the drill until wood dust and smoke start to come out of the hole.

10. When you see smoke coming out of the hole push and pull the bow faster and harder. The wood dust will fall into your notch and onto your tinder. When smoke starts to come from your pile of tinder, you have made a 'coal'. Gently blow on the smoke to produce a flame.

11. Now you have a little fire, you can add some small sticks, followed by some bigger ones until your flame looks stronger. You can then build your campfire around it using larger pieces of wood.

Top Tip: Hold your bow horizontally and your drill vertically. A pinch of sand in the hole under the drill will create more friction, and therefore more heat. If there are two of you, take it in turns to bow, so that your wood powder doesn't cool down while you are taking a breather.

SURVIVAL SKILL WARNINGS:

It is extremely dangerous to start a fire. Always follow the advice below when starting a fire in a survival situation:

- Keep a container of water or soil at hand in case you need put out your fire quickly.

- Choose a suitable spot for your fire, away from anything that could catch alight, such as trees, bushes, dry grass and buildings.

- Make sure that all your belongings are right out of the way and remove any stones from the area – they could get really hot and shatter.

- Always keep an eye on the fire to make sure it does not get out of control. When you have finished, make sure you put the fire out and that no embers are left glowing.

HOW TO SURVIVE A FAMILY CHRISTMAS

Forget alien or zombie attacks, studies have shown that there's nothing more alarming than your extended family invading for the Christmas holidays. Seriously, take a leaf out of this book and ensure your own survival.

Check what time your relations are due to arrive and offer to pop to the shops for last-minute supplies at that exact moment. This may not be ideal – no one likes shopping – but you will avoid the 'meet-and-greet' stage. This is the time when your head is patted, your cheeks are pinched and you are buried under an avalanche of hairy-chinned kisses to cries of 'Haven't you grown?'

Take advantage of having lots of people in the house and run for cover! In the middle of all the hubbub you'll find it much easier than usual to slip away unnoticed and have some time to yourself. Hiding behind the Christmas tree is an option, but may prove a tricky, not to say a prickly, manoeuvre. Instead, take a torch, some bite-sized snacks and a good book and head for your room. The wardrobe or under the bed make excellent hiding places.

IF ALL ELSE FAILS

Make a plan with your friends to meet up at the cinema or to go bowling on Boxing Day. You need excellent persuasive skills to achieve this, as you have will probably have to be excused from a variety of family activities. Siblings wanting to tag along can be a particular problem.

Think ahead and have a decent bribe prepared to prevent your brother or sister pointing out the unfairness of you escaping, the house or asking to go with you.

Top Tip: Keep your ears open at all times for any announcements regarding presents. You must not miss out on the best part of the festivities just because you were busy making your escape.

Surviving Christmas involves a lot of running around and it can seriously take it out of you. So listen out for meal times and make sure you fill up on all the seasonal goodies on offer to keep your energy levels high. Your parents may tell you not to be greedy, but you'll get plenty of support from your granny, because you are, after all, 'a growing boy'.

HOW TO WADE THROUGH RUNNING WATER

Wading through water – especially fast-flowing water – can be very dangerous. So the rule is: never wade unless you absolutely have to – for example, you are being chased by a water-hating wild animal and you simply can't get around the water, there's no bridge or boat, and you've no means of building a raft. Do not wade through water that is higher than your knees.

PICK YOUR SPOT

- Make time to look at the stretch of water you're planning to cross, and if there's time find out as much about it as possible. How deep is it? How fast is the current? Are there any obvious shallows, sandbanks, islands, low overhanging tree branches or large rocks that might help you cross?

- Choose the best crossing site you can. Look for the area with the shallowest water and the gentlest current. Current travels faster on the outside of a river bend than on the inside, so avoid outside bends. It is very tricky to tell how strong the current is just by looking at the surface of the water – however, the shallower the water, the less force the current will exert on you as you wade. The pressure of fast-flowing water on your legs will come as a shock at first and it will increase as you edge deeper into the water.

- Look for a stretch of river where the banks are low. That way it will be easier to get in and out of the water.

- Very cold water can be extremely dangerous, as it will affect your body's ability to function. Never attempt to wade through water that is too cold.

OVER AND OUT

1. Make a 'wading staff.' This should be a strong, straight stick, cut to about the height of your shoulder. If possible, make a wrist-loop from string or cord and lash it to the staff about 20 cm from the upper end. This will stop the staff getting lost if you drop it.

2. Take your trousers off, but keep your boots on. You will need them to grip the riverbed and they will protect your feet from anything sharp underwater.

3. Undo the belt of your backpack so that you can remove it quickly if you lose your footing while crossing.

4. Try to keep your belongings dry. Make a raft for your clothes and kit from a waterproof sheet. Put a bundle of sticks and some straw in the centre of your sheet (to create some air pockets), pile your trousers and clothes on top, then tie up the bundle with cord. Attach it to your belt. When the time comes, carefully float the bundle in front of you as you wade across.

5. Use your wading staff to test the riverbed and the depth of the water ahead of you. Even shallow places may have deep potholes, and there are often unseen obstacles such as hidden rocks or waterlogged branches, or sudden patches of sticky mud or sand. The staff will also help you to keep your balance. If possible, and provided the current allows, use any exposed sandbanks or large rocks as resting places during your crossing, allowing you to make it in a series of short 'hops'.

6. Aim to take a route that will take you across the river diagonally upstream, to another low bank. Face upstream, into the direction of the oncoming water. Turn your body so that you are inching your feet sideways across the river. Do not take steps, as though you are walking – shuffle your feet under water, one step at a time, using the staff to help you stay upright.

7. Don't hurry, and don't make any sudden movements. If one boot misses its footing, use your staff and the other foot to recover your balance.

8. If you lose your footing don't panic. Lie on your back and let the current take you, feet first, downstream, using your hands as paddles to guide you into shallow water where you can stand up again.

SURVIVAL SKILL WARNING:

Wading through water is a skill that should not be used when your street floods. In everyday life you should never wade through water that is higher than your ankles. Stick to wading through your bath water. You know how deep it is in there.

HOW TO MAKE A DUG-OUT CANOE

One day you stumble across a big fallen tree in your garden. Why not suggest your family works together to make a dug-out canoe from the tree, by digging out the wood from the tree trunk? You can demonstrate your amazing survival know-how and test your skill of matching different people to different tasks. You will gain serious credibility.

CHOP, CHOP!

1. Cut the branches from the fallen tree. Give this job to a big, strong, grown-up family member. Then ask them to saw off the length of trunk that will form your canoe.

2. Next, select someone to remove all the bark from the trunk.

3. When the trunk is bare, look carefully at how it is shaped and decide which end will be the slightly pointy front of the canoe called the 'prow'. Before turning the trunk over to begin digging out the wood, you need someone to shape the prow. It needs to form a gentle point that will cut through the water when you are paddling.

4. Next, get all your family members to work together to gently turn the trunk over. Wedge it firmly, to stop it rolling.

5. Before you begin digging out the interior of the canoe, mark out where the sides will be by scratching some marks in the wood. That way your team will only chop out wood that is inside that mark. If everyone works steadily for several days, the inside of the canoe will begin to appear.

6. Collect the chopped-out wood and put it in a safe place so it can be used as firewood.

7. As the wood is chopped out, the inside surfaces should be carefully shaped and smoothed so the sides are the same thickness all the way round.

FINISHING TOUCHES

When work has finished on the inside, roll the canoe over together and finish shaping the outside, chopping away any lumps to cut down the weight of your canoe. Use sandpaper to smooth the smooth surface so it will glide through the water.

The last job is to make the canoe waterproof both inside and out. Some dug-out canoe-makers use boiled tree resin, which they spread over the wood. However, there are boat-building oils and varnishes which will do the same job and are much easier to use. Waterproof the canoe all over.

Dad will be itching to try out the canoe on some water as soon as the last waterproof layer is brushed on, but it is up to you to make him wait until the canoe is completely dry inside and out.

Don't let anyone be too ambitious on the first outing and set off on a trip abroad. Plan a short trip in calm waters. Dug-out canoes need to be paddled gently.

If the canoe feels a bit wobbly when everyone is inside, you can fit small supports called 'outriggers' either side. These are hollowed-out lengths of wood, attached to the canoe by poles. When these are fitted securely, they will balance the canoe and reduce the chance of it tipping over.

Finally, you'll need paddles and floats. A cushion each will give members of your family something comfortable to kneel on while they are paddling.

Bon Voyage!

Top Tips: Be careful how your family chops out the wood. If they cut too close to the edge of the tree trunk they could weaken the side or bottom of your canoe, or worse still, put a hole right through it.

Ask them to cut notches across the trunk so that the chunks of wood between them can be chopped out more easily.

Remain patient at all times. Making a dug-out canoe will take a long time, but it will all be worth it when the family can paddle their canoe down the river.

SURVIVAL SKILL WARNING:

Never try to make a dug-out canoe by yourself. For one thing it will take you about a year, and for another thing, you run the risk of chopping up your finger instead of chopping up the tree trunk.

HOW TO BE A MODEST HERO

Display heroic behaviour at all times, but always be modest. Remember:

• Actions speak louder than words. Always do your fair share of the really unpopular tasks so that everyone can see you are prepared to pull your weight.

• Give your seat to older people on buses or trains – it shows you are both kind and considerate. Help an old lady safely across the road whenever you can (but only when you're sure she wants to be on the other side).

• No matter how much your arm hurts after falling out of a tree (having saved a kitten from certain death), brush aside offers of help or sympathy.
Say things like 'It's nothing,' or 'I'm used to this kind of pain.'
Cry later when you get home – your mum won't tell anyone. You'll always be a hero to her.

• Never boast. True heroes are quiet and unassuming. Play down all your achievements. If other people want to sing your praises, just shrug or shake your head as if you are embarrassed by the attention.

HOW TO SURVIVE YOUR TEACHERS

School survival skills are among the most important skills you will learn in this book.

TEACHER TYPES

There are many types of teacher. Some think they are too cool for school and wear wacky waistcoats, and then others – who know there is something you would much rather be doing – give you a mega-impossible project to do anyway. You suspect they would prefer it if you handed in the work late so they get to tell you off.

TEACHER'S PET

It doesn't matter what your teachers are like, the following tips will keep you in everyone's good books.

• Be on time. This sounds boring, but teachers hate it when you are late and will use it as an excuse to pick on you for the rest of the day. Getting in early means you won't be put on the spot later when you might not have been paying attention.

• Remember the excuses that work. If you hear your teacher shouting at a friend because they claimed the dog ate their homework, don't use that one yourself (even if it did). Make your excuses long and complicated. Hopefully your teacher will be bored by the time you get to the end, or even better stop you halfway through and just tell you to bring in your homework tomorrow.

• Show some enthusiasm. Teachers find this encouraging and it makes the lesson go much quicker. Ask intelligent questions or request help when you need it. This shows that you want to learn and that you're not just sitting there waiting to go home.

• Everyone gets caught talking in class at some point. If this happens to you, you need to think quickly about what you were supposed to have been studying and claim that you were talking about that. Taking time to look up a relevant subject at the beginning of the class can save you detention time later.

HOMEWORK AVOIDANCE TACTICS

Now it is time for an advanced survival skill – homework avoidance. This should only be attempted if you are confident of success. For best results pick a Friday afternoon class. Teachers, believe it or not, are as tired of school as you are on Fridays, so are vulnerable to this prank at this time. About 20 minutes before the final bell, put your hand up and ask a question. You must choose this question carefully. It must be relevant to the subject, but require an incredibly long and complicated answer. Here are some examples:

Maths. 'I read that people didn't always have minus numbers or zero. What did they do before that?'

History. 'Do you think that in two thousand years' time they will describe our era as the Middle Ages?'

Your teacher will, if you are lucky, be very impressed by your curiosity and will ramble on answering it until the bell goes, completely forgetting to set your homework for the weekend.

Top Tip: Don't overdo it. Putting your hand up first and finding everything your teacher says fascinating will impress your teacher but not your classmates. Always remember you are trying to survive your teacher, not be asked to sit with them at lunchtime.

ALSO AVAILABLE . . .

The Girls' Book: How To
Be The Best At Everything
ISBN: 978-1-905158-79-9

The Girls' Book of Glamour:
A Guide To Being
A Goddess
ISBN: 978-1-906082-13-0

The Boys' Book: How To
Be The Best At Everything
ISBN: 978-1-905158-64-5

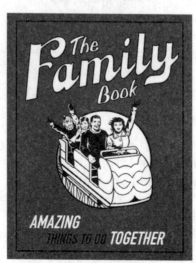

The Family Book:
Amazing Things To Do Together
ISBN: 978-1-906082-10-9